Singing

the

Gamut

Singing
the
Gamut

A Motley Clutch of Poems and Verse

RAYMOND H. HAAN

RESOURCE *Publications* · Eugene, Oregon

SINGING THE GAMUT
A Motley Clutch of Poems and Verse

Resource Publications
An Imprint of Wipf and Stock Publishers
199 W. 8th Ave., Suite 3
Eugene, OR 97401

www.wipfandstock.com

PAPERBACK ISBN: 978-1-5326-8249-0
HARDCOVER ISBN: 978-1-5326-8250-6
EBOOK ISBN: 978-1-5326-8251-3

Manufactured in the U.S.A.   APRIL 18, 2019

To the memory of Miss Helen Zandstra,
my English teacher in grade twelve,
who brought the sunshine of encouragement

Contents

Preface

THIS COLLECTION OF POEMS and verse reflects the gamut of my varied thoughts and recollections during the course of about a year. The only organizing element is a loose seasonal arrangement; I have not attempted to provide uniformity of subject or mood. Some poems may be poignant or introspective; others are whimsical and intended as mere diversion. My addiction to music requires that the words sing as the ideas travel the gamut, for poetry without music is a bird without song.

I give necessary and eager thanks to Dr. John Van Dyk for pushing me to publish some of my work and to Kathleen Herrema for reading the manuscript with precision, appreciation, and insight. My wife, Claretta, and my daughters, Julie Bennett and Mandy Lohman always provided patience and understanding, for which I am grateful. I am grateful, as well, to my grandson Daniel, who sometimes gave readings of these poems after dinner—and did so, perhaps, for even better reasons than to escape drying dishes.

The Original Gamut

(Some Details for the Curious)

IN THE MUSICAL TERMINOLOGY of the Middle Ages the *gamut* designated two things: the bass note G an octave and four notes below middle C and the range of seven scales built on that low G. The final note of the seventh scale was the note E, ten notes above middle C. By extension *gamut* has come to mean the span or range of anything.

The syllable *gam* of *gamut* (bass G) comes from the Greek letter G, *gamma*. The second syllable, *ut*, was the word for singing the first note of a scale. It was later called *do*. So, if someone sang the scale starting on low G (called *gamma ut*), he began with the syllable *ut*, singing thus: *ut, re, mi, fa, sol*, and *la*. (Early scales had six notes, not eight, as our scales have.) In short, *gamut* derives from the Greek word *gamma* and the Latin word *ut*, meaning *so* or *thus*.

More Details for the Compulsively Curious

The Italian Benedictine monk Guido d'Arezzo (990?-1050?) devised the gamut in order to help singers remember the scale. He did that by writing a plainsong melody for the Latin hymn *Ut Queant Laxis*, beginning the first syllable of each musical phrase on a successive note of the scale, so that *ut* was G, *re* was A, *mi* was G, and so forth. Here are the words and the famous syllables that Guido d'Arezzo used to help his singers remember the ascending notes of the hexachord, the six-note scale.

E	**la**bii reatum.
D	**So**lve pollute
C	**fa**muli tuorum,
B	**Mi**ra gestorum
A	**re**sonare fibris
G	**Ut** queant laxis

Winter Solstice

Doxology for the Happiest Day of the Solar Year

The day is grey,
its hours are brief,
the sun's away,
there's no relief
from endless clouds
that hang like shrouds.
The sky seeps grief.

And yet below
that grey and cheerless pall,
the souls who take no joy in snow,
who have endured the sad decline of fall,
and who have sorrowed at the sun's ordained demise,
with quickened heart and furbished hope tomorrow may arise:
though winds may howl and cold may chill, though ice may cling, and snow may blow,
now *sol* stands still, poised to return. To God let soul-filled solstice praises flow!

Where All Past Years Are*

The years dissolve from view
like a ghost train,
each year a phantom boxcar
    (containing portraits of happy faces at weddings,
    crying and cooing babies,
    children shouting at play,
    a schoolroom, an office, a church,
    Thanksgiving and Christmas dinners,
    sweaty work, awful scenes of anger,
    tender moments of love,
    screams of pain, shouts of euphoria, funerals,
    cars, pets, houses, friends, parents, children).

Away glides each memory-haunting phantom,
boxcar after ghostly boxcar, down the narrow track of time into
the numb night of forgetfulness.
Off they go to tease the mind, to torment the spirit,
dwindling quickly with their cradles and their coffins,
their hovels, their houses, their headstones.
Away they wheel down the solitary track,
dwindling, ever dwindling, into grey oblivion,
into the faraway realm of things unreal,
of things subsumed at last into nothing more than
boxcars of a ghost train,
laden with lonesome, groping memories.

*John Donne, "Tell me where all past years are,"
from his poem "Go and Catch a Falling Star"

Times Square, December 31
(The Symbol and the Devotees)*

This night the naked, newborn year,
  in dry and downy diaper clad,
floats far above the crazy crowd—
  appearing both aloof and glad.

The throngs below, in frenzy loud,
  (before the crystal sphere descends—
long, long before their vigil ends)
  have gently** moistened their Depends.

*I learned today of the woeful plight of enthusiasts who come early in the morning to Times Square to insure their places at the descent of the spectacular new year's ball—and of the discomfort that their devotion causes them throughout the day, owing to the lack of portable comfort stations.

**Human experience being wonderfully varied, it would be presumptuous to assume that this is the proper adverb. In fairness, therefore, let us list a few other realistic possibilities, remembering that in this context (and perhaps in New York City) the action of the celebrants is regulated by meter:

slowly	wildly,
quickly	fiercely,
meekly	warmly
weakly	fully

Orientation

Tonight I walk, companion to the shining moon.
The moon, to keep its lofty distance, sails straight on—
to every quirk and quibble of this world immune.

Aloof, it makes its flight through frigid skies,
remote from earth, where lunar gender wrangles rise:
"La lune! woman moon," the Frenchman cries;
"Der Mond, a manly moon," a German voice replies.

And so, throughout this starry, cloudless night,
the wise white sphere soars far aloft, and, being bright,
it pours a pure and penetrating light
onto our strange and darksome mortal gender plight.

For, shining clear, this brilliant sphere becomes our tutor:
accepting of its orb, obedient in its orbit,
not masculine or feminine, but wholly neuter.

Invocation

My mind, like a clothes dryer,
after long revolutions,
after venting needless heat,
comes to a momentary stop.
Sorting through its contents,
I discern colors and fabrics
but nothing whole, nothing complete;
for all is tangled, knotted,
and quite reluctant to be made
separate and smooth.

Spirit who moved upon the waters' face
when earth was void and formless,
reach into my twisted, thick disorder,
draw out its fabric to plain view,
untangle, sort, and smooth chaotic knots;

bring to me needful order, clarity, release,
and make a worthy place of tidiness and peace.

Pub Philosopher

Froth bubbles, rising thick on beer,

enjoy a bright but quick career:

they fizz, they burst, then disappear.

"We've lost our heads," the tippler quips.

"Oh, well, that's life," he says—and sips.

Magi

Astrologers, perhaps, like mulish Balaam,
or like spiritual descendants of Joseph or Daniel,
sapient and strong to pursue the wondrous star,
they come—mysterious, mercurial as the star itself;
like Sheba's queen they come,
known, yet unknown, bearing lavish gifts.
Low they bow for a perpetual moment
beneath the gaze of the omnipotent infant—
beneath His lavish gift to all wise men:
one white and welcoming star.

Slowly, then, they turn and, dreaming,
follow God from Bethlehem
into their own land.
And still they trek through the deserts of our imaginations,
kindling visions of God's real and dream-like plan.

Having been first to bend to Him below,
will they be first, as well, to bow to Him above,
leading the way on dazzling dromedaries—
leading our prodigious gentile train
to view the risen King's resplendent majesty?
Will they be first to kneel, to gasp, to marvel,
and to hymn His glory in euphoric praise?

Political Truth

(The Comfort of Pliability)

The politician's gifts are rare:

his mind is keen, keen is his eye.

He thinks, then winks: "I must declare,

    to me it seems

    between extremes

    the supple truth can aptly lie."

A Shrinking-Word Poem

S   n   o   w

n   o   w?

No!

Perspective

In secondary splendor,
borrowed majesty,
the mist-whiskered moon
illumines earthly gloom
and mutes the brilliance
of every bright and mighty star.

Gloria Patri

Curved cherry arms lift
white praise of moon-lit blossoms:
pure, silent glory.

Computer

It's just a *thing*:

passionless, inflexible, unyielding, unsympathetic.
Its program must be *your* program; *its* limitations must be *your* limitations.
Mutely, obstinately,
it reduces one
to servility,
to frustration,
to wrath—
even to visions of vengeance.
Did I buy it? Yes.
Is it useful? Yes. Oh, yes.
And addictive? Ah, yes.
And helpful? Yes, of course, helpful.
But it's only a *thing*, a mere *thing*
without one soft part:
no blood, no thought, no heart—
insensate,
cold, cold, *cold*,
never pliant.
all-defiant,
a mute and tyrannical giant
of a *thing*—a mere *thing*
that behaves like a dogmatic, despotic, doggone *king*.

Seed

This small, winged seed,
whirling uncertainly to its place,
this drifting embryo,
long-descended seed of Eden's stock,
may grow dry and dormant,
guarding the dark and lively mystery
of its ancient, implanted power;
and yet, with sunlight borne on gentle wind,
with sweet baptismal rain,
with the embrace of nurturing earth,
this wafting embryo may swell,
may burst, may spring up,
and may bring forth progeny prodigious—
as did Abraham.

Clocks of Spring

The clocks of spring have wheels and gears,
the speeds of which (so it appears)
have small relationship to time,
but move aloof, detached, sublime.

It seems the robins want to wait
this year until the snows abate.
But daffodils, whose hopes abound,
send slender spears through frozen ground.

The crocus, warmed by slanting sun
thrives long before the spring's begun,
and peepers peep down in the mud
before the blushing redbuds bud.

The Maker of internal clocks
gives every wren and frog and phlox
a secret timepiece of its own,
to herald news that winter's flown.

So, Maker of my waning clock,
I trust Your timing to unlock
the winter of each earthly thing
and quicken me to timeless spring.

Modesty

Bloodroot clothed in white,
crocus in mauve,
daffodil in yellow,
tulip in multi-hued beauty,
redbud in regal glory,
cherry and crab in bridal splendor,
assert their triumph over winter—
in silence.

Today's Lesson

After their death
blossoms of the lilac send up, still,
a scent of ineffable sweetness,
having exercised in life absolute obedience
to their Maker's will.

Robin

Pecking in grassy weed beds
and sifting through thickets,
you gather dry grass and small sticks,
about half your body's length,
no, not a mere score—
but three hundred and more.

In the labyrinth of a friendly tree
you find a limb, secure, protected,
where you pile your hoard of sticks and grass.
Soon you work them into a circle,
weaving with your beak
and shaping with your feet and body.
Then you bring mud in numberless beakfuls
to bind your work together
and fix it firmly to the tree.
Having lined your nest with mud
and tamped it smooth all round
with fast-pattering feet,
you finish with soft fibers, grass, and hair
for eggs and nestlings to be sheltered there.

You have no need for tools
besides your beak, your feet, your breast;
and flawless plans within your tiny brain are stored,
engraved there from creation by creation's Lord.

When all is finished, you look down.
A man strains on a ladder to hang
his square and newly-painted birdhouse,
made with wood and screws and glue,
built with saw and plane
and screwdriver and paintbrush,
designed from a clever internet plan
devised by some clever internet man.

You have no call to wonder
at its bizarre unbirdliness.
Your masterpiece accomplished,
you need only to chirp contentment
from the top of this tree (the tallest one)
in the waning warmth of the golden sun.

Hygienic Hints

(Seasonal Signals)

When the curled worm wriggles
in the robin's beak,
when the muskrat giggles
near the splashing creek,

when the warm rain sprinkles
on the newborn foals,
when the lawns get wrinkles
from the paddling moles,

when the air breathes fragrance
from the trees and flowers,
when the begging vagrants
seem to like spring showers,

then a call comes clearly
to the souls who care:
"It's the time for yearly
change of underwear."*

*One of the patients at Pine Rest used to say, "This is the time of year to change your underwear." That might have been an old logging camp expression—or practice. One might think, though, that waiting for so many months might have been stretching it.

Separate Worlds

The sticky worm writhes
in the nesting robin's beak;
a house finch trills bliss.

Look!

Even the white moon
has sailed out to glory in
this delicious day.

The Visit

My dream was of the visit Jesus paid
to this, my very house. With care He laid
aside His shepherd staff and splendid crown.
Owner he was, not guest, as He sat down.

With Him came peace; we had no thought of fear,
and I, because His presence was so dear,
was quick to hear and serve Him as I should
and in my service offer all I could.

My labor was not hard; each act was joy,
for deeds and thoughts were wrought in love's employ.
No aim had I of payment or reward,
for all my heart was bent to please my Lord.

> My waking brought
> (or so I thought)
> an empty chair.
> No staff lay there;
> I found no crown,
> no royal gown,
> no presence dear,
> to shield from fear.

"How easy, Lord, would be my thankful task
if in your very presence I could bask.
If clearly I might see the One I serve,
how little from my service I would swerve."

Then quick there seemed to come a chiding voice,
a gentle voice, dividing rule and choice:
"Remember these words both by day and night,
my child: *We walk by faith and not by sight.*"

Dignity

Naked Adam sought with leaves of figs
to find some part of dignity again.
Generals and admirals in uniforms,
pontiffs and priests in vestments,
politicians in dark suits and stuffy shirts,
citizens in working clothes—
all find in dress some refuge,
some respect, some comfortable dignity.
So it is in the doctor's room or hospital,
when we regain the refuge of our clothing.

The cross brought Jesus cruel indignity.
Naked before His world He hung,
the pure hanging before the impure,
the object of shame dying for the shameless.
Naked he hung
to array His fallen world in fresh and perfect dress,
naked
to clothe His chosen ones of Adam's flesh
in seamless robes of white and righteous
kingly dignity.

Mr. Van Ginkel and the Brown Cloud

Lynden, early 1950's

In the bright field we worked,
next to the clear-flowing waters of the Nooksack.
Four or five of us toiled in the barley or hay harvest,
heaving the sweet-scented bales onto the wagon
or building sun-burnished shocks with barley sheaves.
Early we came, conveyed by farmer Van Zanten,
rotund, pipe-smoking father of many,
world-wide purveyor of daffodil and tulip bulbs,
and owner of a widespread, thriving farm.

We awaited his arrival on fresh mornings,
standing on a quiet corner of the sleepy streets,
expecting his ancient, lumbering station wagon.
We waited, a mostly speechless trio:
I, the youngster of the group, half bashful and a trifle mischievous,
Maas, a man of fading middle age and touchy temper
(who once knocked my quart Thermos bottle to the sidewalk when I teased him),
and Mr. Van Ginkel, seemingly ancient, mustached,
habitually pinching a nip from his yellow Peerless pack,
rarely spitting, a miser of words and smiles.
We stood, waiting on the corner: one young boy in summer clothes
and two tired laborers in their ragged overalls and flapping jackets,
like figures in a Norman Rockwell painting.

In the bright field we labored and sweat.
Sometimes a school friend worked with us,
and always farmer Van Zanten's older son was there.
Our lunches stayed behind till noon,
but farmer Van Zanten brought a precious gallon jug of clear water.

It was like the common cup for communion in church—
you drank in faith that former lips were pure
(or maybe you never thought about labial purity).

Of course, we conspired to drink before
Mr. Van Ginkel came to the jug,
for after his long pull a foul brown cloud
floated in the precious water
like a wispy picture in a cheap kaleidoscope.
Then my friend and I drank, like Gideon's soldiers,
from the cold and snow-fed water of the Nooksack.
In those days germs held small concern for us:
they had the decency to be invisible—on the jug or in the river.
But Mr. Van Ginkel's brown cloud had no disguise.

A Cautionary Tale

about a garage mouse, whose carnal desire controlled his mind and corrupted his spirit, who, therefore, never achieved adulthood, and whose end was wretched beyond imagination

Quivering whiskers!*
Shelf after shelf,
boxes and boxes
all for myself:
boxes for nests,
boxes for babies,
safe from foxes
who might have rabies;
old tables and chests,
arrows and bows,
jars in long rows,
all sorts of house tools,
(no trace of mouse stools),
old chairs and bags,
a table, all black,
for human massage,
bags crammed with rags,
cans for the ease
of plant disease,
squash in a sack,
reeking of mold—
and, also, I'm told,
(if I am plucky
and truly lucky)
a morsel of cheese,

*See the end for extensive notes.

served on some flappy,
snappy contraption
in the fall of every year
for some mousely belly cheer.

Ah! cheese, Oh! Cheese.
One dreams of seas
of fragrant cheese,
luscious, yellow,
sharp or mellow,
wholly smooth or
smooth and holey,
heavenly cheese,
rapturous cheese,
celestial cheese.
My soul agrees
that I need cheese,
cheese freshly cut
right off the butt.

Though it might sound droll,
I need not control
my cholesterol.
And no salt or lactose,
or colon impactose
causes me unease.
So, if you please,
bring on the cheese.

But wait!
What do I hear
far in the rear?
It's mice, I fear,
who have come to claim
the very cheese
for which I came.

The scent of cheese
wafts strong and clear.
I drool, I loll,
I pant, I wheeze;
I cannot control
my aching desire.
My soul burns with fire
for Parmesan cheese!

But what is this?
There sits Fred,
and there's Susie
(Fred's never choosy)
and pups in a brood—
all very snug, all very smug.
But that's not just *food*,
THAT'S CHEESE!
They're sweet and snug,
feasting in bliss
on my very food.
From what I can tell,
it's a mouse hotel
they're sitting in.
Grin after grin,
as smug as you please,
it's MY CHEESE they're eating.
That needs repeating:
it's MY CHEESE they're eating.

They've stolen my cheese,
and that's a sin;
yet they'll slice me thin
if I come in.
Since that is so,
away I go.
Fate never sends
to make amends.
No cheese, no friends,
head hanging low,

Oh! Oh! away I go.
Addicted,
conflicted,
away I go,
head hanging low,
no luck, no lovely cheese, no friends—
and fate will never make amends.
So now I make my plan to die
and very slowly putrefy;
and it will be my carnal pleasure
to rot and reek beyond all measure.
I'll ooze and waft a Roquefort scent
to make the people here repent.
And as they ask, "Who cut the cheese?"
I'll fester, leak—and, later, freeze.
This my epitaph should be,
plain for all the world to see:

    EPITAPH:
    Here lies Mouse; be silent, please.
    He was a most unlucky critter:
    the social structure made him bitter.
    Young he died, deprived of cheese.

    His dying wish:
    May swarms of fleas who have disease
    infect all those who took MY CHEESE.

*Notes on "A Cautionary Tale"

1. Detailed research indicates that the parents of this mouse were church mice. It is, therefore, odd that he did not seem to enjoy the benefit of having been christened. Unreality being what it is, his parents most likely named him Pewbert after the location of his birth: the padded pew of a local church. Our research shows his full name to be Pewbert T. Mus (Mus being the name of his genus, and T standing for Tertius, third in the litter). We hardly need to elaborate on the apt correspondence of his name to his adolescent condition. The moral depravity of this immature creature, as seen in his epitaph, makes us wonder about the social influences in his life. He was bred and born in auspicious circumstances, that is, he was the son of a church-going family and had the unique benefit of being delivered into the very pew of a church. We feel confident that future researchers will discover him to have been the victim of evil companions and corrupting social or political influences.

2. Our minute and unflagging inspection confirms that the description of the garage in this story represents the very garage of the author in every detail, except for very slight additional material, which he has gratuitously supplied for verisimilitude.

3. Pewbie's expectations are easily plausible, and consequently we must accept them as genuine. As with all other details, the incidents in the story itself have been vigorously verified—except for the ending, which is visionary. The ending, therefore, rises nobly above the need for mere physical corroboration. In this respect the accuracy of the story supersedes either news reports or government documents, which, unhappily, have been known to fall somewhat short of infallible. Incidentally, we should add that the political leanings of Pewbie, though obvious, are somewhat puzzling.

4. A note on the rhyme of this poem: Mice are known to have trouble keeping regular rhymes, but, being compulsive, they insist that every line must rhyme somewhere. (We should observe that Pewbie failed to rhyme a couple of words, but those omissions are undoubtedly the result of his remarkable artistic acumen and design—and his resolve to avoid vulgar compulsion.)

Sweetness

(Peoria, Iowa, 1944 or 1945)

On that idyllic Iowa morning
the owner of the old general store
had sold me candy,
twenty-five cents worth of candy—
enough candy, it seemed, for a monarch and his queen.

Sweet was that candy,
sweet the stroll with the little princess
(from two houses down in our village),
sweet the songs of meadowlarks
in the burgeoning ditches,
sweet the warmth of sunshine on the gravel road.

Oh! sweet—until Mr. Dahm, the owner of the store,
informed my father of my purchase—
astounded him that I had squandered a quarter—
a whole quarter—on candy.

Yes, I did confess to having secretly withheld that quarter
from the offering plate on the Sunday past.
And, of course, I had to work two weeks to pay it back.

But still, the joy and abandon of that moment,
the sweetness of sunshine and summer green,
the singing of the meadowlark,
and the communion of candy
remain lifelike and lively in my mind.
It was like the beginning of the world;
it was like the first spring of all springs.
It was rapture.

That picture is imperishable:
it could as well have happened this morning.
Ah! I wish it had.

Have a Nice Day!

Maybe we can talk again sometime.

Diplomacy, politics:
two concepts that
thrive in the practice of
public servants, board presidents,
principals, corporate operatives,
advertisers, bankers and stock brokers,
lawyers, panhandlers, and swindlers.

Politics, diplomacy:
they embrace one plan of operation,
they hold one common goal.
So close are they that (we might say)
they take lunch together—
my lunch.

Waste

Independence Day

Would that every shining sparkler,
every snapping or thunderous firecracker,
and every flaming fountain of fireworks
were a prayer,
an impassioned petition
for the mercy of God
on this tottering nation.

An idea

is an eclair:

sweet to the mind,
but
gone in a flash.

Reality

Having your head in the clouds
invites danger:
unexpectedly
the pit bull Life
will take
a jolly big bite
out of your
flop-

py
fun-
da-
ment.

Stillness

Wea VanderVeen Buurma,

27 September 1868—21 November 1940

I do not recall the trip to Kalamazoo from Wellsburg, Iowa,
and I do not recall the funeral.
I hold a single memory of my grandma.
It is the first memory of my life,
a memory without color, without scent, and without words.
It is merely a picture of a child,
left behind in the living room
after all the others have gone to the kitchen—
a child who in perplexity and curiosity has
climbed up onto the coffin
and who sits in stillness,
wondering at the deep stillness of Grandma.

First Funeral

Henry Ipema, my classmate, about 1947, Chicago

In scratchy Sunday clothes I sat with my classmates from grade four,
sat in awe and fear, only a few feet from Henry's open coffin.

Henry had drowned in Lake Michigan,
and there he lay before us,
eyes closed, unmoving.
Though his casket was buried in flowers,
I saw and sensed only ugliness.

No doubt the organ played,
no doubt the preacher preached—maybe even to us children.
I remember only that someone sang "God Leads His Dear Children Along"
with its refrain, "Some through the water, some through the flood."

Besides Henry's body three other things cling to my memory:
the flies, the flowers, and the scent.
The busy flies, eager, perhaps, for flowers and for the flavor of death,
buzzed through the open doors on this hot day,
found the welcome scent of Henry, and feasted on his defenseless face.
They landed on us, too, and on the panoply of flowers,
repugnant in their thickly-mingled scents.
Mostly, though, I was overwhelmed by the awful proximity of death—
the unwanted nearness of the body of my friend:
his wrong-colored skin, his unnatural, ghastly inertness.

Against this I had no defense: I could not push it away, I could not hide from it.
Surely I was vanquished in this early skirmish with the last enemy.

Air Brakes

"Phillip, stop! *Stop!*"
I wanted to shout
as I turned the car into the driveway.
But no words came.
I was too late, anyway:
he was running down the garage roof,
a four-year-old with no idea of danger, no sense of fear.
He was running down the garage roof
with nothing to stop him,
with no one to catch him
if he fell toward the concrete below.
He was running straight down the garage roof—
and at the very edge he came to an abrupt and upright halt.

The angel was invisible,
but his work was marvelously plain.

He shall give his angels charge over thee
to keep thee in all thy ways.
They shall bear thee up in their hands,
lest thou dash thy foot against a stone.

—PSALM 91:11, 12

Moss

Proud flaming sumac,
send another leaf to burn
on my green altar.

Song

Black notes fill the staff:
lines of sparrows punctuate
this dawn's deep-orange song.

Henry Ford

(1863—1947)

Defunct and Debunked

"History is bunk," the magnate said.
    His words became immortal;
though we who quote and read them
    now suppress a skeptic chortle.

For as our minds retrace his phrase,
    we long to ask: "If it be true,
O venerable and clever Ford,
    what part of all that bunk are you?"

Men's Morning Coffee

"Well," he said, setting down his cup
and struggling with both hands to stand,
"at least we can be confident
that Providence is on our side in all this turmoil.
At my age you begin to realize
what a lucky thing *that* is."

The Liturgy of Departure

After the ineffable elevation of spirit,
after the expansive final chord,
when the sound-breathing wind has ceased to
evoke glory from the pipes,
after the faithful hearers have come
with handshakes and hugs,
after the lights are put out and the doors are locked,
then begins the liturgy of departure
for the organist of fifty-three years.

Muted light sifts through stained-glass windows,
pale purple and lucent blue,
engulfing the pews and quiet aisles.
The building sleeps; its nightly gasps and creaks begin.
Alone in the sacred semi-darkness,
the organist resumes the time-worn bench.
Trance-like he sits, then gently, as in a dream,
he draws the stops to make such sounds
as bathed bereaved and stricken hearts
with peace throughout the tumbling years.
He plays—he knows not what—until, at last, his spirit,
full to overflowing, pushes him to the threshold of farewell.

Now holy dusk obscures his form.
He bends, only for a moment,
near the inert companion of his soul,
gently lays his keys in the promised place,
lingers numbly before the purpled pews,
and finally forces his steps toward
the Janus-faced uncertainty of retirement,
engulfed in emptiness for his insensate but responsive friend
and for the blessed balm of sound that bound them together.

Evening Prayer

My spirit is a garment, hanging, torn.
With sharpest, gentlest needle, Lord,
now mend me,

that wholeness from your hand may give, come morn,
some help and wholeness where you choose
to send me.

Furniture

Nine years ago Julie returned after the divorce,
came with a garageful of household paraphernalia
and precious furniture, moved from faraway Alaska.
Then came little Daniel with his toys and books—
his home-schooling, and his tormenting fear of abandonment.

"Our lives will change," I had warned.
"Nothing will be the same."

They came to the downstairs of our small condominium,
and crowded in with all their needful things.
Not much order was possible, nor tidiness.
We had to move the furniture about—
the couch, the desk, the chairs and cabinets.
Only my beloved grand piano stayed in its place.
Upstairs we moved the furniture, too,
for Daniel's vision therapy equipment.

Time went by, congestion diminished,
Julie began working, Daniel went to school,
and the downstairs was quiet for hours at a time.
Now Julie's business is growing, and she works more hours;
Daniel, now strong and confident,
goes away for school and tennis and karate.

On Sundays and most evenings they are both downstairs.
Their voices echo up the steps,
and we talk from floor to floor.
When it is quiet, I can sense their presence.
All of that feels right; it feels solid and reassuring:
they *should* be there—

they should *always* be right there,
in the messy downstairs on the misplaced furniture,
because, after all,
they are an immovable part
of the furniture of my heart.

Predestination

As the caterpillar pads his silent way across the sidewalk,
his supple brownish body blocks the rays of the setting sun,
forming a black and bulging shadow on the warm cement.
He marches steadily forward,
carrying beauty in his color, his movement, his determination.
He marches steadily forward
without pausing to contemplate his shadow or anything else,
and soon he disappears into the grass and detritus lining the sidewalk.
He seems girded with purpose, focused on the groundwork
for that euphoric day when he will no longer crawl—
that rapturous day when he will no longer be *able* to crawl.
Maybe, deep within his furry being there tingles
a sense of his glorious time to come.
Maybe even now the sweet urgings of instinct
are whispering in his caterpillar ear,
murmuring of mysterious transformation,
whispering of paradisal wings and deft, idyllic flights.

Supplication

*Those that be planted in the house of the Lord shall flourish
in the courts of our God. They shall still bring forth fruit in old age;
they shall be fat and flourishing.*

—PSALM 92:13,14

Loathing its wilted thinness,
this aged plant recalls its flower and fruit—
and shudders at inevitable desiccation and decay.

Great Gardener, let me not grow lean and fruitless.

Grant me some watering,
some reviving, or, perhaps—
perhaps—a gentle transplanting.

Easy Refutation

God has, some say,
a sense of humor.
But I say, No,
that's just a rumor.
I'll tell you why
in reverent tone:
no spirit has
a funny bone.

Science Lesson

Now, children, contemplate the Blob,
the wondrous protoplasmic glob
that slid or wobbled from the ocean,
brought into being by the motion
of varied substances and stuff—oh,
perhaps four billion years ago.
At first Blob was an algae speck,
without a spine, without a neck.
It had no eyes, it wore no glasses
but slowly grew mid slime and gases.
No arms it had, no hair to part,
no ears, no liver, and no heart.
Blob could not breathe or show emotion,
it simply sprawled close to the ocean—
much like (although we can't be sure)
an aged cake of cow manure.

Regarding how Blob came to be,
the scientists do not agree.
(Theirs is no work for mental peons,
for Blob was Blob before the eons.
In fact, Blob might have oozed from slime
before the time when there was time.
For time's beginning is a mystery
beyond the marvels of all history.)
But, children, pause to celebrate
the Blob's exalted lowly state.
For Blob in its astounding way
holds records to this very day:
the Blob lived eons by the millions,
and Blob showed patience through the billions.

Yes, science makes Blob half eternal,
which makes his patience quite supernal.
For if Blob took twelve million years
to grow the smallest pair of ears,
then what about a brain or liver?
(Such lengths of time can make one quiver.)

So, pity not your first forbear,
who flopped (sans coat or underwear)
beside the sea of liquid goop
that wise men call primordial soup.
For Blob at last became less thin,
became a thing of blood and skin—
became just what *you* are today—
and will, perhaps, remain that way.

But will there come more steps or stages?
Will we evolve in coming ages?
Or will we slide back as a group
into the grey, primordial soup?
A soupward slide would scarcely please,
although it could be done with ease.
In fact, from what we see and know,
the ears and heart seem ripe to go.

Two Memories

Youth

Lynden, c. 1951

Across the creek we swung,
grasping the loop in the strong rope
suspended from a thick limb high above.
Across the creek we swung—
a quick run, a gentle swing,
an easy landing on the other bank.
Even when two people grabbed the rope and swung
(awkwardly struggling, whirling, shouting),
no one ever thought the branch would snap.

Nostalgia

Grand Rapids, 1954

Imagine a sixteen-year-old, coming home after school,
finding in the mail a vinyl recording of Grieg's piano concerto,
unwrapping it, putting the needle on the disc,
adjusting the volume, hearing the music for the first time—
and not getting past the second movement
until he had put the needle down on it five times or more.

As I listen to that music now,
its pathos washes over me again.
Its tender and passionate lyricism
instills the same indefinable longing,
the same empty aching,
the same irresistible melancholy,
the same heart-tugging reflection of a world,
sometimes beautiful, too often sad, and always incomplete.

To a Fallen Blackberry

You were not this morning's choicest berry,
but because I had you in my grasp,
somehow I want you more.

Precariously extended, I stoop and stretch
in my struggle to retrieve you,
now fallen out of sight
beneath the green of jagged leaves,
fallen beneath the mass of tawny brambles,
intertwined and serpentine,
fallen into the purple of decay.

What is it that compels me to seek you?
You are just an ordinary berry, one of myriads,
and I could pick a score or more instead of struggling for you.
Besides, your ruthless thorns have crisscrossed my hands with scratches,
leaving them blood-blotched and rasped
and bristly with your stickers.

Yet I arose before the sun and came to seek you
when the cool dew clung trembling to your trailing vines.
Now in the sun and sweat I struggle in this tangle
you have fallen through to the dark and odorous earth.

For one compressed, expanded moment
I forget the whirring of mosquitos and the torture of my back
as I feel your cool and fragile roundness in my hand.
And suddenly I pause, still stooping, sweating in the bitter brambles,
while something in my heart cries out,
"Do you see me, Lord?"

Upside Down and Backwards
Grand Rapids Christian High School, 1953–1955

Against the window pane,
upside down and backwards,
slowly, patiently, I traced my father's signature
under the counterfeit excuse
I had tapped out on his black L.C. Smith typewriter
(with its happily idiosyncratic defects of print).
The school, with its overwhelming size, its cliques,
and its classroom regimen provided little joy.
Its thronging hallways were to me
but prisons of constriction and loneliness.
So, I gloried in the freedom my forgery produced,
and I took unpardonable pride that
my duplicity eluded Mr. Hoekenga's hawk-like scrutiny
and his righteous arm of discipline.
Yet, looking back through the window of time,
I am forced to wonder
what was truly backwards and upside down.

T e a r s:

optics

most potent for

seeing

the

cross.

Sunset

The recumbent moon
floats like a ram's horn of gold
on bedclothes of fleece.

Hell on Earth

(biking beside the freeway)

The overwhelming roar of engines
and the hissing and pounding of tires on hot pavement:
unearthly hints they are of
the wallowing and hissing of dragons
in the hot and heaving oceans of hell.

October Shroud

Clear skies,
ivory moon.
Frost in numbing darkness
stalks naked autumn blooms, spreading
white death.

The Sepulcher of Winter

Torn yellow leaves litter
the damp, glistening asphalt in moonless gloom.
Trees, spectral, naked,
their branches black and thin,
shiver in the rain-laden wind.

The rebel heart rejects the empty limbs,
cries out against decay and ugly death:
"What beauty breathes in winter's sepulcher?"

A gentle voice sifts down through darkened space,
a voice unveiling both the cryptic face
of changing nature and of changeless grace:

> *Black night gives birth to rising sun,*
> *the balm of solace follows grief,*
> *travail precedes the joy of birth:*
> *all pain is parent to relief.*

> *A dying worm brings forth the moth,*
> *and dying streams thrive in the sea.*
> *Our death leads but to shining birth,*
> *time's death to bright eternity.*

Lines Written for Those
(Especially of Calvinistic Persuasion)
Who Might (or Might Not)
Be Seeking an Ancient Precedent
for Female Clergy

The female moth

was *foreordained*

a woman of the cloth.

Geriatricks

When you've lived long enough to boast about
how old you are, there's small time left
to brag about your age. In short,
the problem with longevity
is its increasing
brevity.

Black   Friday

A composite of the festivities as
reported from year to year

It is no secret that Black Friday
follows turkey-pumpkin-pie day.
Before your pumpkin pie is done,
the Friday raptures have begun.
Before you're finished with your turkey,
half the world has gone berserky.

Stores open early, open late—
times the mobs appreciate.
Stores are decked with Christmas frills;
savvy women man the tills.
"Unlock the doors!" the bosses yell.
"They're howling like the fiends in hell.
It's time the hoards should have their fun.
Stand back! The mob is on the run!"

The mob stampedes, once past the doors;
the building brims with shrieks and roars.
As shopping spirit grows and thrives,
the ardor of the moment drives
some eager shoppers in the throng
(whose wait has been both cold and long)
 to shove or jostle, push or paw,
or utter speech that sounds quite raw
(impelled, of course, by shopping glee,
borne on the wings of ecstasy).

The shopping joys more ardent grow,
and shoppers, grabbing boxes, throw

them lovingly to friends in back.
That action signals an attack
on merchandise of every kind.
Contestants surge up from behind;
contestants in the front defend
their sacred stacks and stoutly fend
off foes with elbow, fist, and voice.
The victors in their strength rejoice—
until fresh waves of sporting folk
come up to shove and swear and poke.
But strong Security arrives.
Their mighty muscle quickly drives
away all sporting joy and thrill—
all triumph with TV or grill.

Above the shoppers' din and roar
from the speakers sweetly soar
Christmas carols of every sort—
which add devotion to the sport
and waft their messages of peace
as carnal shopping joys increase.

When post-Thanksgiving day is past
and shoppers come to rest at last,
we learn from gurus in the news
some facts we really cannot use:
in the frolics mercantile
as shoppers capered aisle to aisle,
some used pepper spray, most not,
some were trampled, some were shot.
In their hijinks some got bumps,
some got bruises, some got lumps,
some got thrown to wall or floor,
some got stabbed in shopping war,
and some got shuttled to the clink—
all because of rich black ink.

One thing the news forgot to tell us
(between the ads for things to sell us):
Black Friday is a dual tradition—
it smacks of profit—and perdition.

Sic Transit Gloria

The Parable of the Eclipse

Pure and perfect monarch of the frigid winter sky,
the moon arises full, in silent majesty,
and reigns tonight in radiant dominion,
its kingdom stretching over earth and heaven.
Here below its brilliance etches on the snow
black shadows of naked, shivering trees.
Its glory, far above, surpasses every lesser light—
until a tiny touch of dust appears
upon the monarch's unsuspecting underside.
That dust creeps imperceptibly, like black fungus,
slowly, very slowly, crawling up the brilliant face,
slowly, steadily, smothering its light,
until the stricken moon, now grown vaguely red,
succumbs at last to fungal pall
and lapses into black obscurity,
a regent, a borrower—
for brightness, shape, and size a mere dependent,
a servant month by month and hour by hour
to circumstance and vastly higher power.

Winter Solstice

This day is an old, old man,
weary, shrunken, grey,
now thin where muscle was,
too weak to push away
dark blankets of the sky,
empty for the scents of spring,
for summer's balm,
for fruited, fragile autumn.
Yet, knowing in its thin, insensate bones,
knowing the power of divine precision—
knowing surely that the springing light
will bring once more the summer fields to flower,
it sinks obediently to its early rest,
an old, old man, bent and grey,
yearning for the growing light—
groaning, even, for perpetual day.

For we know that the whole creation groans and travails
in pain together until now.

—ROMANS 8:22

www.ingramcontent.com/pod-product-compliance
Lightning Source LLC
LaVergne TN
LVHW050047090426
835511LV00033B/2796